KIRKLAND

JUL   2010

21st
Century
Skills Library

ANIMAL INVADERS

MONITOR LIZARD

BARBARA A. SOMERVILL

CHERRY LAKE
Publishing

Published in the United States of America by
Cherry Lake Publishing, Ann Arbor, Michigan
www.cherrylakepublishing.com

Content Adviser

Dr. Sarah Simons, Executive Director, Global Invasive Species Programme

Credits

Photos: Cover and page 1, ©Dawn LeBlanc/Alamy; all other images used under license from Shutterstock, Inc: page 4, ©Ingvars Birznieks; page 6, ©clearviewstock; page 7, ©Roy Palmer; page 8, ©kkaplin; page 11, ©Ashley Whitworth; page 13, ©EcoPrint; page 14, ©Stacy Barnett; page 16, ©dirkr; page 18, ©Matt Paschke; pages 20 and 26, ©Peter Wollinga; page 23, ©steve estvanik; page 24, ©Ilya Shulman;

Map by XNR Productions Inc.
Please note: Our map is as up-to-date as possible at the time of publication.

Library of Congress Cataloging-in-Publication Data

Somervill, Barbara A.
    Monitor lizard / by Barbara A. Somervill.
        p. cm.—(Animal invaders)
    Includes bibliographical references and index.
    ISBN-13: 978-1-60279-627-0
    ISBN-10: 1-60279-627-0
    1. Nile monitor—Florida—Juvenile literature. 2. Introduced reptiles—Florida—Juvenile literature. 3. Nonindigenous pests—Florida—Juvenile literature. I. Title.
    QL666.L29S65 2010
    597.95'96—dc22   2009026012

Cherry Lake Publishing would like to acknowledge
the work of The Partnership for 21st Century Skills.
Please visit *www.21stcenturyskills.org* for more information.

Printed in the United States of America
Corporate Graphics Inc.
January 2010
CLSP06

TABLE OF CONTENTS

CHAPTER ONE
REALLY BIG LIZARDS 4

CHAPTER TWO
**ALL ABOUT MONITOR
LIZARDS** 8

CHAPTER THREE
**IT WAS SUCH A SWEET
BABY** 14

CHAPTER FOUR
PROBLEMS WITH MONITORS . . . 18

CHAPTER FIVE
**CAN FLORIDA GET RID OF
MONITORS?** 24

MAP 28
GLOSSARY 30
FIND OUT MORE 31
INDEX 32
ABOUT THE AUTHOR 32

CHAPTER ONE
REALLY BIG LIZARDS

An elderly woman lives alone in her cottage on the west coast of Florida. She hears a strange scratching sound on her roof. At first she thinks it might be birds or a neighborhood cat. She runs outside to find the cause of the scratching. Instead of a prowling cat, she finds a 7-foot

It could be very frightening to encounter a wild monitor lizard.

(2.4 meter) monitor lizard. She calls the local animal rescue team. Catching the lizard won't be easy. Monitor lizards are extremely strong. They have sharp teeth and foul tempers.

On Sanibel Island, near Florida's coast, a prowler raids a sea turtle nest. Like most **species** of sea turtle, this one is **endangered**. The eggs in that nest represent hope for the sea turtle species' survival. For every 1,000 eggs laid, only one hatchling lives to become an adult. The prowler is not concerned. It is a hungry Nile monitor lizard, and it will eat almost anything.

LEARNING & INNOVATION SKILLS

It takes time for people to realize that an invasive species has become a problem. When monitor lizards first appeared in Florida, they did not seem like much of a threat. Now people know that the lizards are **reproducing**. More lizards mean more problems. **Biologists** are studying the behavior of monitor lizards in Florida. They will use the information to make a plan to get rid of monitors. How do you think scientists go about gathering this information? Can you think of ways this information will help them come up with a plan?

Nile monitors do not normally live in Florida. **Invasive** species such as the Nile monitor are a danger to local plants and animals, including humans. These lizards are fierce **predators** that will eat just about anything. They compete with native predators for food. They also attack endangered species. What happens if they do not find easy **prey**? The lizards will raid garbage or eat dead animals. They may even attack family pets.

A hungry monitor lizard will eat whatever it can find.

Monitor lizards have become a major problem in many areas of Florida.

CHAPTER TWO
ALL ABOUT MONITOR LIZARDS

Monitor lizards are native to Asia, Africa, and Australia. There are dozens of species of monitors. They come in a wide range of sizes and colors. Komodo dragons

Komodo dragons are extremely large and very dangerous.

belong to the monitor lizard family. So do water monitors, Nile monitors, and Savannah monitors.

Different kinds of monitor lizards live in different environments. Like all **reptiles**, monitors are cold-blooded animals that warm themselves in the sun. They can adapt to cold weather regions by **hibernating** during colder months.

Florida has been invaded by the Nile monitor, or *Varanus niloticus*. An adult monitor weighs about 22 pounds (10 kilograms). It can grow to be 4.5 to 7 feet (1.4 to 2.1 m) in length. Its body is long and thin with gray-brown or olive green skin. There are six to nine yellow-gold bands around its tail. The tail takes up more than half the animal's total length. It can be used like a whip.

Nile monitors have a dinosaur-like appearance. Their heads are thick and flat. They have nostrils on top of their heads and two small eyes on either side. They generally burrow along riverbanks, often taking over the home of some other animal. Nile monitors are excellent swimmers, good climbers, and fast runners.

Monitors hunt in the daylight by running after their prey. They bite their prey's flesh with razor-sharp teeth. They also slash with their claws. Nile monitors feed on frogs, snakes, birds, and other animals. They have even been known to eat human **feces**. They are also one of the few animals that will raid crocodile nests and eat the eggs. This tells a lot about how fierce monitors are. Crocodile mothers lay their nests on riverbanks and stay close to protect their eggs. Nile monitors face down crocodiles and successfully take the eggs.

21ST CENTURY CONTENT

Florida struggles with more than 130 invasive animal and plant species. Nonnative insects, fish, birds, and snakes can be found there. Wild pigs and vervet monkeys also overrun the state. Climbing ferns, Brazilian peppers, and Australian pines take the place of native plants and spread quickly. Florida has 48 invasive reptiles, ranging from Burmese pythons to tiny geckos. Invasive species are brought in as pets or decorative plants. Sometimes they come in by accident on ships and airplanes. Florida isn't the only place with invasive species problems. How can we slow the flood of invasive species into Florida and other places? Do you have ideas?

Nile monitor males fight one another to gain the right to mate with females. After mating, the female lays from 7 to 60 eggs. The eggs have soft, leathery shells. The older or larger the female is, the more eggs she lays. Each egg measures about

Monitor lizards have no problem climbing trees to catch their prey.

2 inches (5.1 cm) long. Nests are usually holes in riverbanks, hollow trees beside a river, or termite nests.

The eggs mature in 6 to 9 months with no help from the mother. Once mom lays her eggs, she returns to her normal daily life. When a hatchling is ready to emerge, it uses an egg tooth to break through the shell. Newborns measure 6 to 12 inches (15.2 to 30.5 cm) long at birth. For the first few days, they depend on yolk sacs from their eggs for food. Once they grow a little bigger, they can hunt for themselves. They eat worms, small insects, and snails. The lizards grow quickly. They are ready to have young of their own when they are 2 years old.

Nile crocodiles, martial eagles, and honey badgers prey on Nile monitor hatchlings in their native habitats. In Florida, however, the monitors have few natural predators. More monitors survive to adulthood. The Nile monitor lizard population grows more quickly in Florida than it would in Africa.

The Nile crocodile is one of the monitor's few natural predators.

CHAPTER THREE
IT WAS SUCH A SWEET BABY

In Egypt, changes in a Nile monitor's behavior can warn of a crocodile's presence. For this reason, it may seem like a good idea to have a monitor around.

Many people are still trying to make pets out of monitor lizards.

In the United States, people have other reasons for keeping Nile monitors. They think that owning a monitor is trendy and "cool." It is legal to own a Nile monitor in many states. A hatchling costs about $10 in pet shops or at trade fairs.

At first, it might seem like a great idea to keep a Nile monitor for a pet. The baby lizard is kind of cute. And it is not difficult to feed. It eats crickets and other insects that can be bought at any pet shop. The lizard can live in an aquarium, which is easy to clean.

By the time it is 2 years old, however, that changes. The lizard needs an enclosure roughly the size of a dinner table. Extremely large monitors need even more space. The cage must be cleaned every day. And the area needs to be kept damp. A monitor cage needs a warm area that is about 90° F to 100° F (32°C to 38°C). It also needs a cool area that is kept at about 75°F (24°C). There should also be a basking area that reaches at least 110°F (43°C). Monitor lizards need to be fed mice or rats. All this care becomes very expensive.

In addition, Nile monitors are foul tempered and hard to handle. They see their keepers as threats to their survival. They can attack at any time. They defend themselves with powerful blows from their tails and with their teeth and claws. Bites from Nile monitors can crush bone. Monitors also spray feces at their enemies.

Nile monitor owners often tire of the expense and stress of keeping their pets. When they do, they sometimes look for ways to get rid of their monitors. This can be difficult. Few people will adopt an adult monitor. Most owners are unwilling to kill their pets. Instead, they release their lizards into the wild.

Monitors end up in the wild in other ways, too. Some may have escaped from pet shops or breeders and then reproduced in the wild. Pet shop owners or breeders may also have released monitors. When males become too large to sell or females don't produce young, they are no longer useful. It is too expensive to care for monitors that cannot bring in money.

Several monitors were spotted on the loose in Cape Coral in the 1980s. By 1990, the lizards had a thriving population in the city. Cape Coral's network of canals is an ideal

Nile monitors thrive in the warm, moist environments of Cape Coral.

location for monitors. It gives them a place to swim and banks on which to sun themselves. It also provides access to fish and the nests of wading birds.

At first, people thought the lizards they saw were alligators. For several years, only a handful of sightings were reported. Today, scientists estimate that 1,000 or more monitors live in the Cape Coral area. People find them in swimming pools, in garages, and on roofs. Many pet cats and small dogs have disappeared.

 **21ST CENTURY CONTENT**

Cape Coral is located on the west coast of Florida. This area and neighboring communities are trying to deal with the invasive lizards. Local leaders are concerned for the safety of citizens. One way that leaders help the community is through education. Towns distribute brochures about how to recognize and guard against Nile monitors. They warn pet owners to keep their pets inside. Towns also have emergency numbers to call if anyone spots a Nile monitor. How do you think citizens can help their communities deal with invasive species?

CHAPTER FOUR
PROBLEMS WITH MONITORS

P ilots at Homestead Air Reserve Base near
Miami, Florida, keep a close eye on the landing strip. Nile
monitor lizards have invaded the base. They like to sun themselves on the runways. The reptiles create a serious hazard.
Jets landing or taking off can be damaged if they run over a
monitor lizard. A crash could hurt pilots and ground workers.

*Nile monitors are large enough to disrupt
the course of a jet on a runway.*

The U.S. Department of Agriculture's Wildlife Services helps handle wildlife found on the base. Agents try to capture monitor lizards before they cause any damage. Homestead is more than 100 miles (161 km) southeast of Cape Coral. The presence of monitor lizards at Homestead means that the lizards now live in a larger area than they did 20 years ago. The monitor lizard population near Homestead is not nearly as large as is the population near Cape Coral. Experts expect this to change.

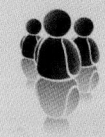

LIFE & CAREER SKILLS

Would you like to work with wildlife? Volunteering at a park is one way to see if you might be interested. Volunteers greet visitors, give tours, and help park rangers remove invasive plants. They must learn about the plants and animals in the park. They may also help keep areas clean and attractive. Students can receive training by working as **interns** in many state parks. Many parks have age limits. Contact a park near you to find out about volunteering.

Nile monitor lizards have invaded the lower third of Florida. They can be found from Port Charlotte eastward to Port St. Lucie and south to the Florida Keys. The giant lizards have also been spotted along the east coast almost as far north as Jacksonville. There is no reason to think that monitor lizards will not continue to move northward. The lizards could easily adapt to the swampy coastlines of Georgia, Alabama, Mississippi, Louisiana, and Texas. There have even

Florida has plenty of water for monitors to enjoy.

been sightings of monitors in California. Those sightings have been few.

Monitor lizards enjoy warm climates where there is water, shelter, and food. Florida's lakes, rivers, and canals provide the water. The lizards find shelter by digging their own burrows or by invading the burrows of other animals. Food is plentiful because monitor lizards will eat just about anything.

West coast Florida residents have many concerns about the presence of monitor lizards. So far, there have been few reported human injuries. Still, people are worried about letting children play outside.

The giant lizards can also be a traffic hazard. In their native habitats, they sun themselves by lying on rocks or riverbanks. They like heat, and Florida's roads provide rock-like surfaces and plenty of warmth.

A major concern is the effect that Nile monitors will have on the native animal population. Florida has 118 animal species that are endangered, threatened, or "species of concern." Nile monitors present a threat to many of these species. They hunt in the water and on land. They will even climb up trees to attack roosting birds.

Scientists are most worried about American crocodiles, several species of sea turtles, gopher tortoises, and burrowing owls. All of these animals build nests on the ground. Their eggs are a treat no monitor lizard would pass up. The monitors devour eggs and destroy the nests. They also eat newborns in the nests.

21ST CENTURY CONTENT

The Convention on International Trade in Endangered Species of Wild Fauna and Flora (CITES) is trying to help stop trade in wild animals. Every year, billions of dollars are spent transporting live animals, animal parts, decorative plants, and medicines that come from endangered species. Trade in these items is illegal, but many people ignore the laws. They do not care about the damage done to the environment. Taking monitor lizards from Africa is just one of the actions banned by CITES. The lizards are among more than 30,000 species of animals and plants protected by CITES. Why do you think people continue to capture and sell endangered animals?

Efforts to trap the lizards are only partially successful. Although the lizards weigh only about 22 pounds (10 kg), they are fierce fighters. It takes at least two people to handle a large adult monitor. Trappers must wear protective gear. Captured adults lash out at their cages. They hiss, spit, and flick their

It is easy to see why people need special clothing to protect themselves from monitor claws.

blue-black tongues at their captors. The difficulty of handling monitor lizards is just one more problem to be faced as the lizards increase their range in Florida.

CHAPTER FIVE
CAN FLORIDA GET RID OF MONITORS?

N o action was taken for several years after the first Nile monitors were sighted near Cape Coral. People who ran trapping services received only a few calls to trap lizards. Citizens sometimes reported sightings to their town governments or local animal rescue agents. There were few

Even though scientists have been able to capture a large number of monitors, thousands are still running wild in Florida.

events involving monitor lizards. Most people didn't think a serious problem existed. They were wrong.

In 2003, biologist Dr. Todd S. Campbell began studying Nile monitors. Campbell reviewed 200 reports of monitor sightings in the Cape Coral area made between the years 2000 and 2002. For the next 2 years, Campbell and his crew surveyed the Cape Coral area. They looked for lizards, burrows, tracks, and other evidence of lizard activity.

Citizens were encouraged to call the Cape Coral Field Office and report any signs of monitor lizard activity. The office handed out press releases with information about the dangers of monitor lizards. Newspapers and television news shows worked with the field office to keep residents informed.

The number of sightings reported increased in response to this information. Calls came in at all hours of the day and night. The field office had only a handful of workers to answer them. If several reports pinpointed a specific site where monitors could be found, field workers placed traps to catch the lizards. Traps were large, metal cages baited with rotting squid or fish. The foul smell attracted the lizards. About one lizard was caught each week. The team set out 20 to 30 traps per day and worked 2 to 4 days a week for more than 1 year. From July 2003 to May 2005, more than 100 lizards were captured.

Florida law allows for captured monitor lizards to be **euthanized**. The lizards are taken to veterinarians and killed painlessly. The lizard bodies are then packaged and frozen.

Later, scientists study each of the bodies. They examine each animal's health. They also determine its gender, age, weight, and the food it ate. Scientists hope that this information will help them create a plan to get monitor lizards out of Florida. So far, no such plan exists.

The field office team ran into several problems in their battle against Nile monitor lizards. Trapping is a slow process. The Nile monitor population increased more quickly than the trappers could catch them. Eventually, the field team ran out of money.

Nile monitors will probably continue to cause problems in Florida for a long time to come.

Florida's conservationists want to get rid of Nile monitor lizards. It is going to be a hard job. Monitors have slowly spread out over large areas in the state. They adapt easily to different habitats. Adult monitors produce many hatchlings. The hatchlings grow quickly, become adults, and produce more young. Can Florida rid itself of monitor lizards? It is possible. But the effort will require a large staff, a huge amount of money, and support from the public. While all of these things are being organized, the lizard population keeps growing.

21ST CENTURY CONTENT

Being part of a community means considering what is best for all citizens, businesses, and the environment. On one side of the lizard situation are the concerns of homeowners, **conservationists**, and public officials. These people want to save native species and think that euthanizing the monitors is an effective solution. On the other side are citizens who support animal rights. They believe that killing the lizards is cruel. What do you think is more important—the survival of Florida's native animals or the rights of Nile monitors? Why?

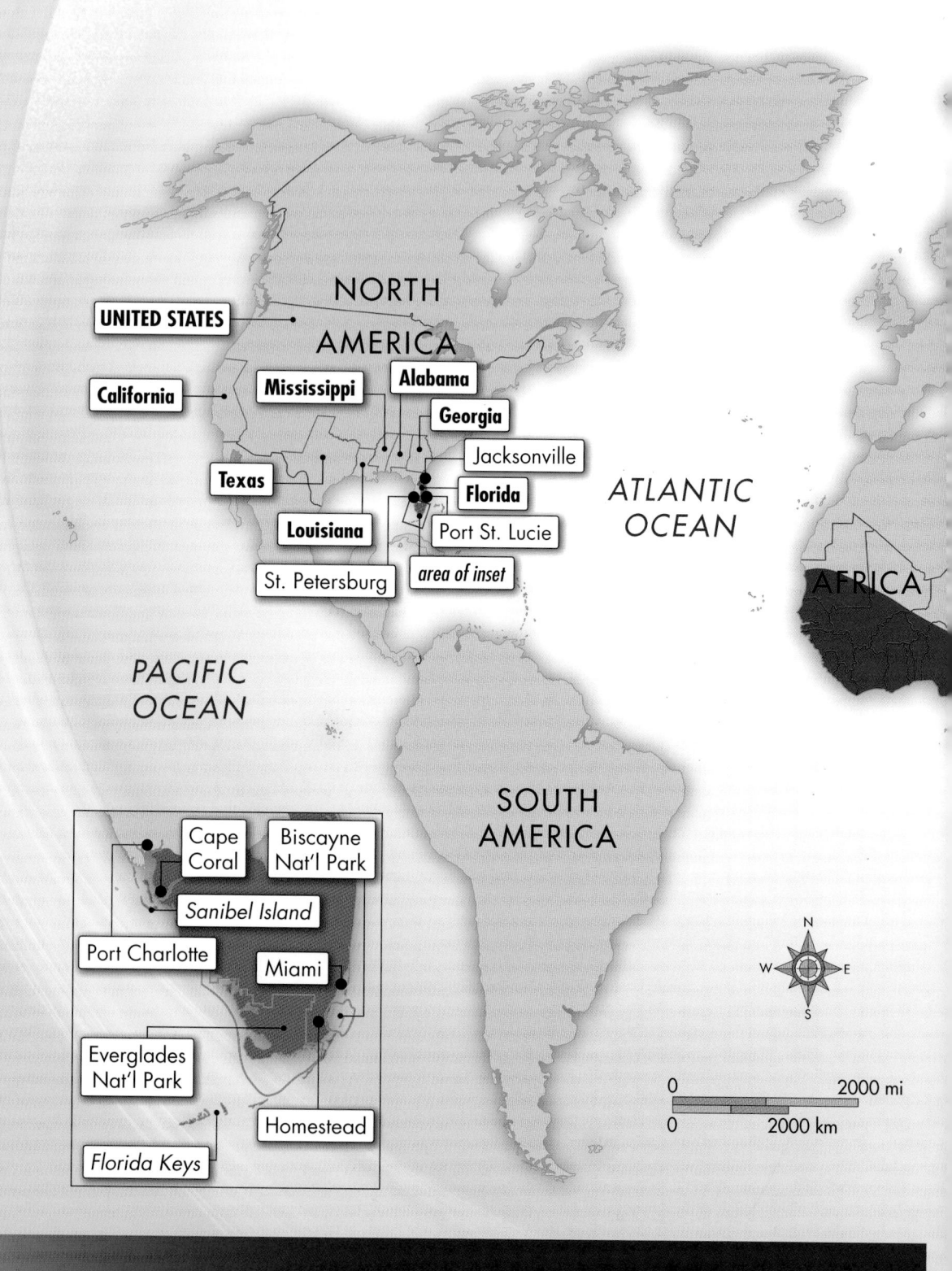

NORTH
AMERICA

UNITED STATES

California

Mississippi

Alabama

Georgia

Jacksonville

Texas

Florida

Louisiana

Port St. Lucie

St. Petersburg

area of inset

ATLANTIC
OCEAN

AFRICA

PACIFIC
OCEAN

SOUTH
AMERICA

Cape
Coral

Biscayne
Nat'l Park

Sanibel Island

Port Charlotte

Miami

Everglades
Nat'l Park

Homestead

Florida Keys

N

W   E

S

0		2000 mi
0		2000 km

This map shows where in the world Nile monitor lizards live naturally and where they have invaded.

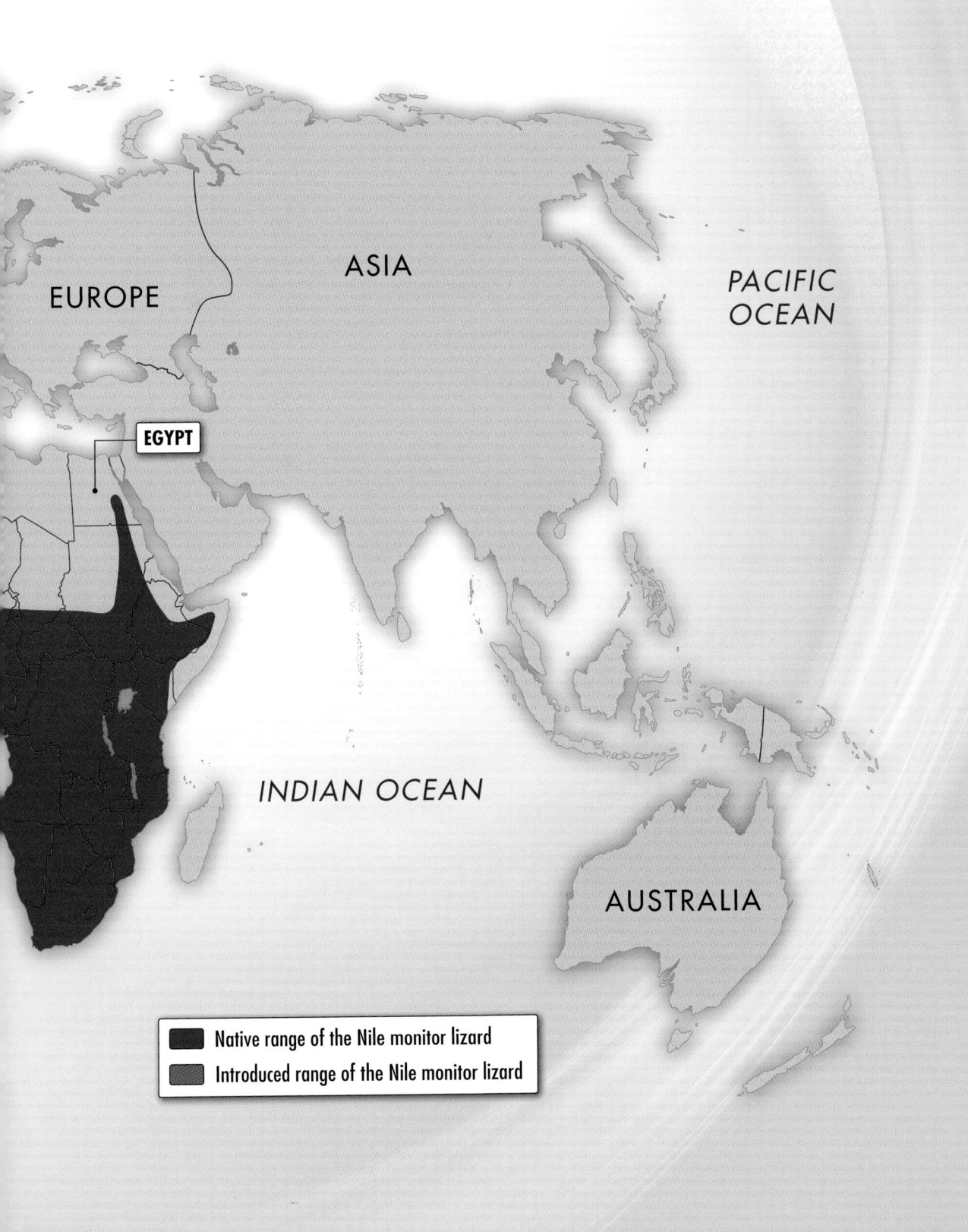

EUROPE

ASIA

PACIFIC
OCEAN

EGYPT

INDIAN OCEAN

AUSTRALIA

Native range of the Nile monitor lizard
Introduced range of the Nile monitor lizard

GLOSSARY

biologists (by-AH-luh-jists) people who study plants and animals

conservationists (kon-sur-VAY-shuhn-ists) people who work to preserve plants, animals, and natural areas

endangered (ehn-DAYN-juhrd) at risk of becoming extinct

euthanized (YOO-thuh-nyzd) put to death painlessly

feces (FEE-sees) solid animal waste

hibernating (HY-bur-nay-ting) spending the winter in a safe location, with greatly slowed bodily activities

interns (IN-turnz) students who receive training through active experience

invasive (in-VAY-siv) having moved into a new area and taken over

predators (PRED-uh-turz) animals that hunt and eat other animals

prey (PRAY) animals that are hunted and eaten by other animals

reproducing (ree-pruh-DOOS-ing) bearing young

reptiles (REP-tylz) cold-blooded animals covered with scales or horny plates that breathe with lungs; snakes, lizards, and crocodiles are reptiles

species (SPEE-sheez) a particular type of plant or animal

FIND OUT MORE

BOOKS

Collard, Sneed B., III. *Science Warriors: The Battle Against Invasive Species*. Boston: Houghton Mifflin, 2008.

Jackson, Cari. *Alien Invasion: Invasive Species Become Major Menaces*. Pleasantville, NY: Gareth Stevens Publishing, 2010.

Magellan, Marta. *Those Lively Lizards*. Sarasota, FL: Pineapple Press, 2008.

WEB SITES

Enter the Dragons
www.sptimes.com/2003/09/26/Floridian/Enter_the_dragons.shtml
Read a newspaper account of how monitor lizards are affecting the Cape Coral community.

Exotic Pet Animals Run Loose
www.flmnh.ufl.edu/fish/southflorida/news/exotic2004.html
Learn about monitor lizards and other invasive species in Florida.

Nile Monitor Lizards
www.sccf.org/content/42/Nile-Monitor-Lizards.aspx
Discover more about the effect Nile monitors are having on Florida's barrier islands.

INDEX

basking, 9, 15, 17, 18, 21
burrows, 9, 21, 25

Cape Coral, Florida, 16–17, 19, 24, 25
claws, 9, 15
climbing, 9, 21
colors, 8, 9
conservationists, 27
Convention on International Trade in Endangered Species of Wild Fauna and Flora (CITES), 22

eggs, 10, 12
endangered species, 5, 21, 22
euthanasia, 25, 27

food, 5, 6, 9–10, 12, 15, 21, 26

habitat, 12, 21, 27
hatchlings, 12, 15, 27
hibernation, 9
hunting, 9, 12, 21

Jacksonville, Florida, 20

Komodo dragons, 8–9

length, 9, 12

mating, 10, 16
Miami, Florida, 18

nests, 10, 12
Nile monitors, 5, 6, 9, 10, 12, 14, 15, 17, 18, 20, 21, 24, 25, 26, 27
nostrils, 9

population, 12, 16, 17, 19, 26, 27
Port Charlotte, Florida, 20

Port St. Lucie, Florida, 20
predators, 12
prey, 6, 9–10, 21

running, 9

Savannah monitors, 9
species, 8–9

tails, 9, 15
teeth, 5, 9, 15
temper, 5, 9–10, 15, 22–23
tongues, 23
trapping, 22–23, 24, 25, 26

U.S. Department of Agriculture, 19

water monitors, 9
weight, 9, 22, 26
Wildlife Services, 19

ABOUT THE AUTHOR

Barbara Somervill writes children's nonfiction books on a variety of topics. Because she lived in Australia, where animal invaders abound, she finds investigating these "imported accidents" fascinating. Barbara takes conservation issues seriously. She is an avid recycler and an active member of several conservation organizations.